New Vanguard • 136

Churchill Crocodile Flamethrower

David Fletcher · Illustrated by Tony Bryan

First published in Great Britain in 2007 by Osprey Publishing,
Midland House, West Way, Botley, Oxford OX2 0PH, UK
443 Park Avenue South, New York, NY 10016, USA
E-mail: info@ospreypublishing.com

© 2007 Osprey Publishing Ltd.

A CIP catalogue record for this book is available from the British Library

ISBN: 978 1 84603 083 3

Page layout by Melissa Orrom Swan, Oxford
Index by Margaret Vaudrey
Typeset in Helvetica Neue and ITC New Baskerville
Originated by PPS Grasmere Ltd, Leeds, UK
Printed in China through Worldprint Ltd.

07 08 09 10 11   10 9 8 7 6 5 4 3 2 1

For a catalogue of all books published by Osprey Military and Aviation
please contact:

NORTH AMERICA
Osprey Direct, c/o Random House Distribution Center, 400 Hahn Road,
Westminster, MD 21157
E-mail: info@ospreydirect.com

ALL OTHER REGIONS
Osprey Direct UK, P.O. Box 140 Wellingborough, Northants, NN8 2FA, UK
E-mail: info@ospreydirect.co.uk

www.ospreypublishing.com

Glossary

AEC	Associated Equipment Company
AFV	Armoured Fighting Vehicle
AVRE	Armoured Vehicle Royal Engineers
DD	Duplex Drive
DRAC	Director Royal Armoured Corps
DTD	Department of Tank Design
LVT	Landing Vehicle Tracked
MoS	Ministry of Supply
PWD	Petroleum Warfare Department
RAC	Royal Armoured Corps
RTR	Royal Tank Regiment
SAE	Specialised Armour Establishment

Acknowledgements

The author wishes to thank Richard C. Harley for his unstinting help with this
book and for the drawing on page 23.

Editor's note

All images are courtesy of the Tank Museum, Bovington, UK.

CHURCHILL CROCODILE FLAMETHROWER

INTRODUCTION

As a weapon, the flamethrower exercises far more power over the imagination than it can actually deliver in reality. It exploits our most primeval fears and, when mounted in a tank, becomes a formidable psychological threat. This is no new thing; when the Landships Committee discarded their huge Pedrail machine in 1915 it was handed over to the Trench Warfare Department at Porton Down, and they planned to complete it as an armoured flamethrower. In the event nothing came of this and there is little evidence for interest in flame as a weapon until World War II was imminent.

Even then flame was regarded essentially as a defensive weapon and in a very short time some 40,000 Flame Fougasse installations were hidden away in the British countryside, along with Defile Flame Traps and Hedge Hoppers where appropriate. In addition, the Home Guard had mobile flamethrower units in the form of trailers carrying drums of petrol and hand-operated pumps, although these were truly last-ditch weapons. Winston Churchill questioned the flamethrower's defensive capability: in a minute to General Ismay in August 1940, he pointed out that in the event of invasion enemy infantry would not move through disputed territory without having scouts and flank guards posted, so surprise with flame traps might not be achieved. Indeed, if the use of flamethrowers in war proved anything, it was that they were primarily suited to the offensive role.

Reginald P. Fraser's original, mobile flamethrower on a Commer lorry chassis. Never a military vehicle in the official sense, it was the prototype for virtually all such equipment in British service.

ORIGINS

Surprisingly perhaps, in light of later events, huge quantities of petrol existed in Britain in 1940. Stocks had been built up during the immediate pre-war period while exports to the Continent had ceased. Should the Germans invade, these reserves would have to be destroyed and many felt that this was best done in direct action against the enemy. Thus, all over the country, various experiments were taking place, and in a move to concentrate this effort the government decided to create a Petroleum Warfare Department (PWD), which came into being on 9 July 1940.

Two schemes should interest us because they each had a bearing on subsequent events. One was based upon the work of Reginald P. Fraser of London University's Imperial College, who was also a director of the Lagonda car company of Staines. Fraser was developing an annular flamethrower that projected petrol with an outer layer of thickened fuel. This, it was hoped, would eliminate the supposed risk of fire working backwards to the fuel tank. But in fact, since oxygen would not be present here, this could not happen. However, Fraser had an experimental vehicle put together by Lagonda on a Commer lorry chassis that was fitted with a flame-thrower turret.

At around the same time the gifted bus designer and ex-Tank Corps officer G. J. Rackham of the Associated Equipment Company (AEC) was developing a design of his own using a powerful Mather & Platt pump, powered by a Napier Lion engine, to produce something quite awe-inspiring: the jet of blazing liquid was expelled at 750 gallons (3,409 litres) per minute. Fitted into an armoured AEC 6x6 chassis and known as the Heavy Pump Unit, it also featured a smaller projector on a two-wheeled carriage that was carried on the back of the vehicle. This could be manhandled by its crew as far away as the hose would stretch. A suggestion, in one source, that 25 of these big vehicles were built seems doubtful.

Fraser's work at Lagonda was highly significant, as we shall see. Developed from his original Commer prototype, Fraser now designed what came to be known as the Cockatrice, based on an armoured Bedford QL vehicle with flame-projector, 60 of which were ordered for the protection of Royal Naval Air Stations. Six more, on the bigger AEC 6x6 chassis, went to the Royal Air Force for similar work. These were described as the Heavy Cockatrice (Mark IA), but apart from the fact that they could carry more flame fuel there was no difference in performance between them and the Mark II (Bedford) or Light Cockatrice. The Admiralty also ordered a version of the Light Cockatrice that could be dismounted from a lorry and carried aboard a landing craft. The result was the Landing Craft Assault (Flame-Thrower) or LCA (FT). The Cockatrice flamethrower, a sample of which was shipped to the United States, used carbon monoxide as a propellant, employed a rotating weapon mount with elevation to 90 degrees and had a range of about 100 yards (91m). Unfortunately, by the time this equipment was in production the need for it had virtually disappeared. The War

The big AEC Heavy Pump Unit thrills its military audience with a high-angle shot. One demonstration, at Leeds Castle in Kent, caused considerable damage to the garden.

This is the Mark IA Heavy Cockatrice, an odd, asymmetrical vehicle that used the same AEC 6 chassis as the Heavy Pump Unit. The flame-projector turret behind the cab and the two machine guns are worked from an open section at the back.

Office had never shown any interest at all, so mass production was out of the question.

The final attempt to produce a wheeled flamethrower in Britain is attributed to Rackham who, in response to a requirement that armoured car regiments should have their own flame capability, designed the Basilisk, based on the AEC Mark I Armoured Car chassis. It was a strange-looking vehicle: rear engined and with a large armoured body surmounted by a tiny, one-man turret that housed the flame-projector and a BESA machine gun. The commander occupied the turret, so he was the flame-gunner; there was also a driver, of course, and a third man known as the observer, but it is not clear where he was located or what he could observe. The flame fuel capacity was 300 gallons (1,363 litres) and the flame jet was propelled by compressed air. Official documents claim a range of 120–130 yards (109–118m), but one commentator reckoned that the effective range was closer to 75 yards (69m). The prototype vehicle was fitted with a 105hp (78kW) AEC diesel, but the report claims that production machines would have been fitted with a 170bhp engine that would have lifted the speed from 30 to 50mph (48 to 80km/h) but, in the event, it was decided not to include flamethrowers in armoured car regiments and the project was dropped. The Basilisk was apparently never issued with a War Department number, nor tested by the Mechanisation Experimental Establishment (MEE) at Aldershot.

The first tank flamethrowers

The concept of having a tank fitted with a flamethrower goes back to 1938, when the General Staff issued a requirement for a tank with a turret-mounted flamethrower based on the current design of infantry tank, the A12 Matilda. The specification was suitably vague since no such weapon existed at the time, but the flame-gun was required to be co-axial with a Vickers .303 machine gun, capable of firing on the move or with the tank stationary, and have a range of between 200 and 300 yards (188 and 274m). The flame fuel would be carried in tanks mounted externally on the vehicle or in a two-wheeled trailer towed behind. One sentence implies that some

Finished in the so-called 'Mickey Mouse Ear' camouflage, this is a Mark II Light Cockatrice of the Royal Navy on the four-wheel drive Bedford QL chassis. Although unproven, it has been suggested that for some of these vehicles other 3-ton (3.05-tonne) 4×4 chassis may have been used.

sort of pump device driven by one or both of the tank's engines would propel the flame jet, but later it was suggested that slow-burning cordite be used to raise the pressure. The problems created by a turret-mounted weapon can be understood if one considers the design of a rotary junction. The designer has to create something that will permit fuel to flow into a turret capable of 360-degree rotation. The junction has to be well engineered to eliminate any risk of leaks, which would be extremely dangerous in the confined space of an armoured vehicle. The pre-war design work on the Matilda took place at Woolwich under the Superintendent of the Research Department, in what soon became the Ministry of Supply (MoS). However, it is interesting to note that the document mentioned above also suggests that the authorities purchase an Italian flamethrower in order to gain experience.

Rackham's Basilisk armoured on the AEC Matador chassis. The flame-projector is in the turret and it may be that the third crew member, designated as observer, would be located alongside where a periscope head may be seen. If so, his view would be very limited.

The onset of the Blitz in the summer of 1940 saw a number of institutions moving out of London. Among them, the MoS department concerned with flamethrower development found itself transferred to a site at Langhurst in Sussex. At around the same time the PWD, under Brigadier Donald Banks, was established on a disused landing ground at Moody Down near Winchester. Up to this time they had operated in whichever part of the country required their services, but things were now changing. The requirement for a tank-mounted flamethrower had been revived and the two organizations became rivals as each set to work on its own design.

Since the prototypes were not completed for some time and were not tested competitively until March 1942, the actual descriptions can be saved for later, but before other experiments are discussed it may be worth looking at the rival propellant systems. Experts at the MoS, where the original Matilda project had first been considered, still favoured a method whereby pressure for the flame fuel was achieved by slow-burning cordite. Unfortunately no detailed explanation has been found as to how this system worked. The PWD, on the other hand, favoured some sort of gas pressure system such as Rackham had used in the Basilisk although, ultimately, nitrogen was preferred as the propellant.

Meanwhile, as this long-term research progressed, other people were at work upon less sophisticated projects. Among them was Lieutenant-Colonel Martin, commanding 47th (London) Division, who in conjunction with a Mr S. W. Adey produced a device for covering anti-tank ditches with fire, which became popularly known as the Adey-Martin Drainpipe. Developed in response to a requirement for mobile, offensive weapons rather than the static defensive kind, the equipment was mounted on a vehicle of the Universal Carrier family and demonstrated by a crew from the Welsh Guards at the Guards' Depot on Sandown Park racecourse.

There was, at this time, no official requirement for such a weapon and indeed the very future of the PWD was in some doubt, but the vehicle was taken to Moody Down and demonstrated to an audience of senior officers that included General A. D. L. McNaughton, commander of Canadian Forces in Britain, whose enthusiasm for the project effectively saved it.

The original caption claims that this is a Wasp, in action in France. In fact it is a Canadian Carrier equipped with Fraser's Ronson device, demonstrating its powers in Britain. Notice the pipe linking the two tanks at the rear.

At the time of this demonstration, May 1941, the British Army's interest in flamethrowers was limited to the man-pack type.

The Ronson

On 5 August 1941, an order was placed for 17 prototype flamethrowers installed in the Universal Carrier vehicle. The project was handed to Fraser, who based it on his original Commer design. Since the systems were intended for the Canadian Army, it was agreed that Canadian-built Carriers would be used.

A *Précis for Junior Leaders*, issued by the Royal Canadian Engineers, gave basic details of the equipment. Two fuel containers at the back of the Carrier contained 60 gallons (272 litres) of fuel and the propellant took the form of a carbon dioxide (CO_2) pressure cylinder stowed in the front compartment of the vehicle. In fact, every effort was made to keep the interior of the Carrier free for its regular crew so that the pipe, carrying fuel from the left hand of the linked tanks, passed along the

A close up of the same Carrier showing how the Ronson Projector is attached and connected. The 'pass' plate on the front indicates Corps troops but the individual unit cannot be identified.

A Ronson Dragonfly with the flotation screen folded down. Seaworthiness must have been questionable, even in a flat ca A marine propeller was driven off the differential at the back

outside of the vehicle to a pivoting projector on the edge of the front gunner's position, where the operator sat. This projector had a range of about 50 yards (45.7m) and there was sufficient fuel and propellant for about 40 short bursts.

The *Précis* accepted that 50 yards was not much range, but pointed out that the vehicle would be moving at the time and would therefore be difficult to hit. The effect of this mobility was enhanced by the Canadians, who removed the governors from their Carriers' engines and, styling themselves the 'Ronson Cavalry', put on some impressive demonstrations at Moody Down. Orders for 1,300 sets of Ronson equipment were placed in Canada, based on information supplied by the Lagonda company, but in the end no Ronson ever saw active service. Despite fluctuations in interest from the authorities, it seems that Fraser blithely worked on with the project and before long had a new system, with far greater range, on the drawing board, which would be known as the Wasp.

Meanwhile one of the more bizarre British developments was the Dragonfly, which was a Duplex Drive (DD) amphibious variant of the Ronson Carrier. Nicholas Straussler had already produced drawings for a

Fraser's Twin Ronson Churchill Mark II in the markings of 102 Officer Cadet Training Unit, which later became the Westminster Dragoons.
It may have had a short range and carried a limited amount of flame fuel, but with both projectors working this vehicle must have been an impressive sight.

DD adaptation of the Universal Carrier, but there was no requirement. On the other hand, adding a flamethrower to the package might be regarded as a step too far. Some prototypes were built and tested, first on a pond in the New Forest and subsequently in the Solent, but one wonders how well they might have performed in the sea conditions prevailing on D-Day and it is probably a mercy that the project was not taken up.

Diversions

Early in 1942, it seems that priorities changed once again and Fraser was informed that as far as the British Army was concerned a tank-mounted flamethrower was preferable to a Universal Carrier, since it was a lot less vulnerable. He got down to work at once and produced a design that featured two complete Ronson units fitted to a Churchill tank. Work went ahead quickly using a Churchill Mark II tank and, since the modification did not involve any major alterations to the tank itself, the prototype was completed by 24 March 1942.

The projectors were mounted, one either side, on the inner track frames at the front of the tank so that they were visible to the driver and his mate. As with the Ronson, a pair of containers, each holding 30 gallons (136 litres) of flame fuel were located at the rear of the tank, feeding the flame-projectors via pipes running along each side of the hull. Since it would be difficult for one man to control the movement of two projectors they were fixed in place so it was up to the driver, directed by the tank commander, to take aim by turning the tank, while the hull machine-gunner was responsible for firing them electrically. Following a demonstration on 26 March, the Chief of the Imperial General Staff asked Fraser if a single projector with greater range might not be better.

Nothing had been done at this stage to improve the range: it was still 50 yards (45.7m) and presumably two projectors would use up fuel twice as fast so the combat effectiveness of the arrangement would be very limited. At about this time a Royal Tank Regiment (RTR) officer and veteran of World War I, Major J. M. Oke, appeared on the scene. According to the records Oke suggested that instead of fitting Ronson fuel containers to the rear of the tank it would make more sense to employ the reserve fuel tank, which was a standard fitting on early Churchill tanks anyway. If this resulted in an increased fuel capacity it would make sense, but it did not.

An unusual photograph apparently showing two Churchill II Okes newly converted. It provides an excellent view of the armoured cover for the fuel tanks, but the non-standard trackguards were not fitted on service. The second Churchill has its air intakes sitting on the engine deck.

The reserve fuel tank was capable of holding 32.5 gallons (147 litres), not much more than half the capacity of a pair of Ronson tanks. A photograph of one of the converted Churchills clearly shows that the tank actually fitted was a good deal larger than the original type, albeit carried in the same way. Whatever the reason Oke must have had more to do with the design than is immediately obvious, since the Ronson-equipped Churchill tanks were known in some quarters as the Oke type thereafter. Some sources suggest that the fuel tank could be jettisoned once it was empty, but this cannot be correct. Photographs taken at around this time show quite clearly that the fuel container and its attendant pressure cylinders were enclosed in an armoured cover, which certainly would not have been dumped when the fuel ran out.

The first Churchill Oke with a single projector was demonstrated on 24 May 1942 and resulted in an order for two more. Impending events were starting to sweep things along and matters were not improved by a certain amount of secrecy and subterfuge. The so-called Dieppe Raid, Operation *Jubilee*, was to include a battalion of Churchill tanks manned by 48th RTR, who commenced amphibious training on the Isle of Wight. It was decided that as soon as they were ready the three flamethrowers would accompany this regiment. In the meantime, however, it had been agreed that the majority of troops for Dieppe should come from the Canadian Army in Britain and an order announced that 'the three Churchill tanks now being fitted with flame-throwing apparatus should be transferred, for operational reasons, from the 48th RTR to the 14th Canadian Army Tank Battalion', the dull alternative title to what was, in fact, the Calgary Regiment.

There is neither space nor need to tell the entire Dieppe story here. Instead it is only necessary to focus on No. 8 Troop in B Squadron, which consisted of the Churchill tanks *Bull*, *Boar* and *Beetle*, all of which were equipped with the Oke flamethrowing device. All three tanks, along with a Caterpillar D7 Bulldozer, went ashore in Landing Craft Tank (2) No.159 on 19 August, but what should have been a significant occasion, the first time British armoured flamethrowers would see action, was blighted by fate. *Bull* was just too eager, launched early and was swamped, *Boar*

Tintagel was with B Squadron, 48th Royal Tank Regiment when photographed as an Oke flamethrower. Here the fue tank is unprotected, but one c follow the pipe as it runs forwa to the projector. T32049 was renamed *Boar* when it went ashore at Dieppe with 14th Canadian Army Tank Regiment

managed to knock off its armoured fuel tank and was unable to use its flamethrower, while *Beetle* got ashore safely and then broke a track.

The story of the Oke ends there; no more were produced and indeed its Carrier contemporary, the Ronson, was also in the process of being replaced. However, it is necessary to bring the tank flamethrower story up to date, and for this we must go back to March 1942 and to Hangmore in Surrey. Donald Banks portrays the event as a cross between a duel of honour and a horse race in which the palm was awarded to the PWD's pressure-operated system.

Both contenders employed Valentine tanks, early models with the 2-pounder gun, but in each case the projector was mounted independently of the main turret. The flame fuel was also carried in a two-wheel trailer towed behind the tanks, but in other respects the vehicles were quite different. The MoS version towed what was known as the Flame-Thrower Trailer No. 3 Mark I at the trial, although photographs reveal at least two types of trailer. The No. 3 Mark I had a capacity of 150 gallons (681 litres) of 'coal tar and petroleum oils', but whether this was a mixture or alternatives is unclear. The operating pressure of 260psi was achieved by the use of cordite, and the system was described at the time as follows: 'a charge of cordite displaced 15 gallons [68 litres] from the fuel tank into a small tank, from which it was discharged through the gun.' Just how this worked is not explained. What we do know is that the flame-projector had a discharge rate of 6 gallons (27 litres) per second, but after each discharge pressure had to be built up again. A simple sum will show that there was sufficient fuel in the trailer for a total of 25 seconds flaming, but this could not be continuous.

The PWD's effort, produced in conjunction with Rackham and Stock of AEC, featured a large, cylindrical tank containing 685 gallons (3,114 litres) of fuel oil carried in an open trailer. Besides the normal towing link, an enormous hosepipe connected the trailer to a large projector mounted on the offside front mudguard of the Valentine. Pressure was supplied at 300psi using compressed hydrogen, which gave a discharge rate of 12 gallons (54.5 litres) per second and a duration of fire lasting 56 seconds, which could be delivered continuously if need be.

Oddly enough, despite the greater pressure behind the PWD system there was not a lot to choose between the rivals when it came to effective range. The MoS system could manage 80 yards (73m) against 85 yards

This is the PWD Valentine putting up a fearsome show, but the trailer is a clumsy affair and the fuel hose curls over the engine deck.

(78m) for the PWD projector. By the curious laws of physics it appears that an accurate balance of pressure with flame fuel and the size of nozzle on the projector were the keys to greater range, not simply increased pressure itself. It is also curious to note a comment, apparently made at the time, to the effect that the trailer towed by the MoS Valentine 'interfered seriously with the movements of the armoured tank'. Why this should not apply equally, if not even more so, to the PWD arrangement is not at all clear.

The MoS contender, with its professional-looking trailer and turret-like projector on the offside, bore all the hallmarks of a finished product. The PWD entry, by contrast, with a crude trailer containing the fuel tank and what looks like a rough-and-ready projector that only appears to fire straight ahead, gave a distinct impression that it was only half finished. Even so, three days later, on 30 March 1942, Sir Andrew Duncan of the MoS announced that the demonstration proved beyond doubt that the PWD system was better and that in future the two departments would merge under Banks. The enlarged PWD would continue development of tank flamethrowers and Reginald Fraser would work on the Carrier variants while offering advice to the PWD. Yet this very confirmation of importance now accorded to tank flamethrowers inevitably involved contact with other bodies, notably, for obvious reasons, the Department of Tank Design (DTD). On 23 June the DTD announced that their preference for future development would be for a flamethrower based upon the Churchill tank, hauling a trailer with either a castor action single wheel or two wheels, something Reginald Fraser had already suggested.

In fact there was so much going on that it was nearly the end of July before authority was given for the next stage to go ahead. The PWD was permitted to order 12 tank flamethrowers for development purposes, only to have the entire project squashed a month later when the War Office Policy Committee announced that it was now only prepared to encourage the development of man-pack flamethrowers and those mounted on Carriers. The reason given was that, in the view of the War Office, no tank could be sufficiently protected to prevent its destruction while a faster vehicle, such as a Carrier, might be able to employ its mobility to avoid getting hit.

To what extent the War Office had been influenced by events at Dieppe earlier that month is impossible to say. After-action reports contained very little of relevance because few of those who returned appear to have

A photo that is not easy to explain; one of three views, none of which are captioned. The vehicle may be a transitional design between Wasps I and II – possibly Reginald Fraser's updated Hornet.

seen the flamethrowers or known much about them. Even so, it seems reasonable to assume that they would have noticed if flame had been employed, so the conclusion must have been that they had failed to get into action. Since success depended upon getting very close to the target, then it could only be that the Churchill tanks, despite their thick armour, had been knocked out before they were within range to flame. This at least would be consistent with the War Office decision, and the theories were confirmed after the war when the survivors returned from the Prisoner of War camps.

Since work on the Carriers was still going ahead, despite previous War Office scepticism, roles were now somewhat reversed. Publicly everyone concentrated on Fraser's very promising Wasp design while a smaller team of enthusiasts quietly went ahead to develop a flamethrowing version of the Churchill that would have greater range – just in case.

The Wasp

The link between Fraser's original design, the Ronson, and the ultimately successful Wasp appears to have been a device known as the Hornet. Fraser first mentions it in a proposal dated 19 March 1942, where it is described as a long-range Ronson. However, another source explains that Hornet involved permanent conversion of the Carrier to the flamethrowing role. Four days later the project was given 'High Priority' and it was subsequently confirmed that 75 Ronson devices would be cannibalized into Hornets.

Fraser must have been working flat out at this time. His Cockatrice vehicles were now being delivered, too late to be of much use; Ronson production was getting under way and he must have been involved to some extent in the various tank flamethrower projects. Even so, the first Hornet was ready in May and at the end of that month Fraser was asked to come up with a revised design that would result in the Wasp. Some time in June the Hornet prototype was burned out during trials and on the 10th of that month Fraser submitted his Wasp design, which is described as a modified version of the original Commer projector that would be a temporary fit.

Clearly, however, the Hornet was not quite dead because on 19 June the chief engineer of First Canadian Army contacted Reginald Fraser and, as a result, staff from the Canadian Petroleum Warfare Experimental Unit (PWEU) were sent to Lagonda at Staines to develop an improved Hornet, which was later demonstrated to General McNaughton. Since no more is heard of the Hornet after this, it must have been eclipsed by the Wasp design. The DTD ordered a Wasp prototype on 12 June followed by an order for 30 on 22 July.

Now that Carrier flamethrowers were once again in the ascendant, another consideration arose. One of the problems of employing a prolific and ingenious inventor is that invariably his quest for perfection leads him ever onwards until he does not know when to stop. Thus, even before the prototype Wasp had been subjected to any trials, Fraser came up with an improved design. Donald Banks had to take a more practical view. Bearing

in mind that a cross-Channel invasion was not out of the question for 1943, he preferred to go with what he had in the form of Fraser's original Wasp design, rather than wait for something new in the hope that it might be better. With hindsight it is clear that this was not the correct decision, since the 1,000 Wasp Mark I units manufactured were only ever used for training, but this was not clear at the time. It is also worth reminding ourselves that since the Wasp, like the Ronson, came as a kit to be fitted to Universal Carriers as required, this did not require large numbers of vehicles to be tied up.

Following yet another change of emphasis from the War Office, it was now decided that it would be better if the flame fuel containers, and indeed all of the equipment associated with them, should be contained within the armour of the Carrier. Thus what was known officially as the Flame-Thrower, Transportable, No.2 Mark I or Wasp Mark I had two cylindrical tanks located on either side of the engine. That on the right contained 60 gallons (272 litres) while that on the left was shorter and held 40 gallons (181 litres), but it shared that side of the vehicle with the pressure bottle and other related items. The flame-gun itself was a relatively large piece of equipment that rose out of the rear hull, rested on the bulkhead that separated the front compartment and poked out over the flame-gunner's head. By packing the rear of the Carrier with equipment there was room for only two crew members – the driver and flame-gunner – and access to the engine was virtually impossible. Worse still, the flame-gun was such a large and conspicuous object that it would be obvious to the enemy, even before it flamed, that here was some sort of weapon a good deal more lethal than a Bren gun, and hence marked the Wasp I as a priority target.

The flame-projector could be traversed, elevated and depressed to a limited extent and, using a thickened fuel, in ideal conditions could squirt out fuel to ranges up to 150 yards (137m). Pressure was supplied by CO_2 and later compressed-air cylinders that, as in the original Ronson, used a heat exchanger to vaporize the propellant. However, although using this system it was theoretically possible to eject the flame fuel in one long squirt, the process developed and patented by Fraser did

View of a Wasp II showing how the two fuel tanks and cylinders fill up the interior. Also shows how relatively inconspicuous the new projector was. This is clearly a demonstration vehicle since it lacks all conventional stowage and any markings apart from the number.

not permit the Wasp to flame in this way. In the original scheme as developed by AEC, ignition at the nozzle of the flame-projector was constant, but Fraser preferred an arrangement whereby the ignition system only ignited once flame fuel was ejected. So, in all Wasp-type projectors, the correct process was to fire short bursts of flame and not one long, continuous burn.

Orders for 1,000 Wasp Mark Is were placed and, as soon as they realized that it was a great improvement on the Ronson, the Canadian Army also took an interest although, as we shall see, they had other designs of their own in the pipeline. Deliveries were completed by late 1943.

Due to the delays imposed by Donald Banks, it was August 1943 before prototypes of the new Wasp Mark II were ready for testing. The projector itself was a good deal smaller than that used on the Mark I, although it had a slightly increased bore. It was also possible to install it in the weapons slot at the front of the Carrier, rendering it a good deal less conspicuous. Yet it had improved elevation, depression and traverse when compared with the Mark I. Another factor that Fraser had to take into account was weight. This steadily reduced, as far as the equipment was concerned, with each successive model. Partly this improvement was connected with handling. The complete flamethrower kit for the conversion of a Universal Carrier came packaged in crates that unit fitters had to handle and install. Thus, the lighter they were, the better. On the other hand, increased fuel capacity meant extra overall weight on the vehicle so any compensatory reduction in material weight was welcome.

Although it was an entirely different discipline within the scientific community, the development of a suitable fuel for flamethrowers was of equal importance and also came under the umbrella of the PWD. Thin, highly inflammable fluids such as petrol produce an impressive result in the form of great billowing clouds of flame and smoke. It impresses the observer, but in reality does relatively little harm. Something thicker that ejects from the projector like a rod of fire not only travels farther but is also far easier to aim and, in the form of an inflammable gel, sticks to what it hits and goes on burning for a while. British and American scientists, working in what might be termed cooperative competition, came up with two solutions that were suitable for use in both flamethrowers and bombs. The British contribution was Fuel Research Aluminium Stearate (FRAS) while in the United States Napthenic and Palm Oil Acid was produced as Napalm. For reasons of security and surprise it was agreed that this thickened flame fuel would not be released for use until D-Day, when it would be employed in another surprise package, the Churchill Crocodile.

Enter the Crocodile

The official decision of August 1942 notwithstanding, the PWD continued work on tank flamethrowers and, in keeping with the DTD preference,

concentrated on the Infantry Tank Mark IV: the A22 or Churchill. Donald Banks admits that progress was slow, for priority had to be given to the Wasp while that was the official favourite. There is some evidence to suggest that work on the Churchill was carried out at the old MoS establishment at Langhurst rather than the PWD's site at Moody Down, perhaps to keep the unofficial project out of sight.

Since this was a somewhat clandestine affair, surviving records are limited, but what evidence there is suggests that the prototype was developed around a Mark II Churchill, the version with a cast turret and 2-pounder gun. It appears to have been completed by December 1942 and cannot have been too secret, as it is mentioned in the Royal Armoured Corps' (RAC) six-monthly report for the second half of 1942, which states that although it was not then a General Staff requirement the PWD was hoping to change their minds by means of a demonstration in the near future. The same report also states that in a recent trial flame had been projected for a distance of 200 yards (182m).

One condition of the project was that it should not inhibit, in any way, the normal fighting capabilities of the tank. As recorded earlier, the DTD had stated in June 1942 that it favoured the idea of a tank with some sort of trailer to carry the flame fuel. A single-wheel, castoring type had already been tested and found wanting, so a two-wheeler based loosely on the old MoS design was developed. It was a substantial item in its own right, armoured to 0.47in. (12mm) standard and weighing in the region of 6.4 tons (6.5 tonnes). The shape will be obvious from the plates. Inside were two large fuel containers which, between them, held 400 gallons (1,818 litres) of flame fuel and five compressed-air cylinders to deliver propellant. There was also a good deal of plumbing and a series of control valves along with a hand-operated pump, in a compartment at the front, that could be used for filling the fuel tanks.

In an ideal world no tank should ever tow a trailer. It is always a nuisance and inhibits the tank's ability to move at will across country, but there are times when it is unavoidable, the case of the Crocodile being one. It was now up to the designers to devise something that would follow the tank more or less anywhere and yet provide an uninterrupted flow of flame fuel and pressurized propellant. The connection between trailer and tank, always referred to as The Link, was a substantial affair as might be imagined. Formed almost as an extension of the front end of the

This is definitely a prototype Churchill II Crocodile and trailer taking part in an official demonstration at Langhurst. Flame fuel trailers used for these early trials lacked the various details seen on those issued for active service.

trailer, it was connected by three large, swivelling joints to a final section that bolted onto the rear plate of the tank. It was, at least in theory, possible for the tank to twist and turn in virtually every direction without upsetting the trailer or doing anything to stop the flow of fuel and gas, but there were limits. If the trailer got into a situation where it was turned either side as far as it could go, and in danger of damaging itself against the rear of the tank, a micro-switch was activated that caused a red or green light to appear in front of the driver, who knew that he could turn no farther, either left or right depending on the light. Also, it probably goes without saying, the tank was quite unable to execute a neutral turn while the trailer was attached. No brakes were fitted to the trailer, nor shock-absorbing springs. For the former it relied on the mass of the tank to hold it in check and it was assumed that the large Runflat pneumatic tyres would be sufficient to cushion the ride at the speeds envisaged.

From the back of the tank a pipe ran down, beneath the bottom of the hull and up through an opening in the floor (normally used to dispose of used shell cases). From here the tube rose up, passed over the hull gunner's right shoulder and entered the base of the projector located in front of the gunner. Although it was hoped to modify tanks to the flamethrower role with as little structural work as possible, it was essential that the front plate, containing the driver's visor and hull machine-gun mounting, be changed. The reason was that in this early design it was intended to make the flame-projector co-axial with the hull machine gun. Maybe this was overstretching the requirement not to interfere with the tank's normal fighting arrangements, but it did mean that the hull gunner, using the same sighting telescope for both, could fire the flame-gun or the Besa machine gun as necessary.

To operate the flamethrower the gunner first had to activate a series of switches, one of which produced a fine spray of petrol from the vehicle's fuel tank. Another set up a circuit for the spark to ignite the petrol spray, which in turn set the main fuel jet alight once that was turned on. With the flame jet ignited the gunner placed with his eye to the sighting telescope, and moving the projector in its mounting he could squirt long bursts in a flaming rod directly at the target or lob small blobs of flame higher to drop behind an obstacle or into a trench.

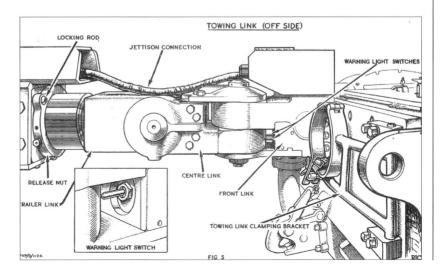

Link: the connection
ween a Churchill and its
er which truly defines the
codile. Inset we see the little
ro-switch that defines the
it of turning.

A Churchill VII Crocodile demonstrates the range and lethal effect of a solid jet of thickened flame fuel, which continues to burn where drop fall to the ground. Squirting fu and setting fire to it afterward was referred to as a 'wet shot

Another method was to first soak the target in unignited fuel and then set it alight with a quick burst of flame. From the victims' point of view it was, by any standards, a terrifying experience to be on the receiving end of a jet of blazing oil. But aiming and firing flame was a slow process and easy to see, so anyone who kept his nerve, at least in the open, stood a chance of avoiding it. Cooped up inside a pillbox under flame attack might be another matter.

Once the trailer had expended its contents, or if it became damaged or caught on an obstacle, it could be disengaged by means of a quick release, activated by a Bowden cable. In theory it was then possible for the tank to continue in action as a conventional gun tank, while the trailer was recovered from the battlefield by a lorry or tractor. To this end the trailer came complete with an additional tow bar that could be fitted at the front and linked to the standard tow hook of a suitable vehicle. Poles were provided that could be used to manhandle the trailer, should the need arise, and a set of tubular legs was also carried, which would support the trailer on an even keel when it was not attached to a tank.

The PWD retained a crew of RTR personnel at Langhurst to man the tank and among those who witnessed one of their demonstrations was Major-General P. C. S. Hobart, commander of the specialist 79th Armoured Division, who would later control the Crocodiles in action, at least vicariously. He is reported as being enthusiastic. However, the key figure at this time appears to have been Major-General Alec Richardson. As Richardson was an RAC advisor to the General Staff, his opinion carried a lot of weight, but he had been overseas at the crucial time when tank flamethrower development was in the doldrums and he was not due to return before December 1942. When he did, and discovered the state of play, he was quite horrified. Banks laid on a special demonstration of the Crocodile for him at Langhurst on 14 January 1943, which clearly made the right impression. On 23 March Hangmore was again the venue for a demonstration for the War Office and, as a result, the project to develop a flamethrowing tank was reinstated in April. Time, however, was running out.

s revealing photograph is
ther mystery. It is assumed
how the prototype Crocodile,
ch employed a Mark II
rchill, but the boss on
near side just above
headlamp suggests
it was once an Oke
clearly not one of
se sent to Dieppe.

Two days after the Hangmore demonstration the prototype Crocodile was taken to Dunwich, where the commanding officer of 54th Division wanted to try out an armoured sledge. This appears to have been an open-topped box, with a hinged ramp at the front like a landing craft and capable of carrying 12 infantrymen. The trials revealed that the sledge could be hitched onto the back of the Crocodile trailer and towed along quite happily, even over rough country and trenches. It may not have been terribly comfortable for the men inside, and one wonders how happy they might have been travelling so close to 400 gallons (1,818 litres) of highly inflammable liquid on a live battlefield, but in the event there is no evidence that it was ever used. However, one other lesson came unbidden from this experience. The east coast of England is renowned for its weather, not entirely to its credit. One demonstration took place in a gale of wind estimated at between 60 and 80mph (96 and 128km/h) and it was found that when it blew as a cross-wind the range of the flamethrower was very much reduced and the jet of flame itself whipped away without ever touching the ground.

The prototype Crocodile was taken over for examination by MoS specialists, since it was appreciated that if any were to be ready for operations the following summer there would be no time to develop an alternative design. Permission to go ahead was given in August 1943 with an order for 250 units, and this before any more prototypes could be produced or troop trials undertaken. Indeed, before production work could begin drawings would be required, most of which would have to be taken directly from the prototype. It was now agreed that the production Crocodile would be based upon the current production Churchill, the 57mm gun Mark IV.

Later in the year plans changed as a new version of the Churchill tank, the A22F Mark VII, was entering production and it was now decided that this, too, should be adaptable to the Crocodile role. At about the same time it was decided to drop production of a new flame-projector in the Crocodile in favour of the tried and tested Wasp unit. This change involved some reduction in maximum range, to about 120 yards (110m)

in ideal conditions, but it was felt that the Wasp already worked so well that there was nothing to be gained by developing yet another weapon. However, this meant that it would now no longer be possible to fit the flame-projector in the hull mounting with a co-axial Besa, so the machine gun was dropped. Since the flame-gun fitted the same mounting it was perfectly possible to replace one with the other as required.

Crocodiles of B Squadron, 141st RAC, which took part in the American attack on Brest. Extra stowage soon got added to the trailers, as well as the tanks. For a while some of these Churchills were fitted with Culin hedgerow cutters.

OPERATIONAL USE

Six prototype Crocodiles were said to be nearing completion in October 1943, but there was still some uncertainty about the arrangements for operating them. It seems that for a while the War Office favoured the idea of supplying the flame equipment to units equipped with the right type of tanks, to be fitted as required, and a complicated drill evolved, at least on paper, to effect this. What it amounted to was that a given regiment would be notified that Crocodile equipment was on the way so that it could start preparing some of its tanks by removing the front armour plate (no mean task in itself) along with the Besa mounting and floor hatch. One trailer would arrive for each tank, towed by a D7 Caterpillar tractor, and this would be parked in front of the tank. Stowed on top of the trailer was everything required to complete a Crocodile, including the new front armour plate. There was some doubt as to whether this procedure really could be done in the field and if it was deemed beyond the capabilities of the regimental Light Aid Detachment (LAD) then it would have to become a Base Workshops task.

Had this practice been adopted then Crocodiles might have operated when required by any Churchill tank regiment in the same way that it was planned to incorporate Wasp Carriers into infantry battalions. This appears to ignore the fact that the Crocodile was a highly specialized weapon, to be used sparingly and requiring a very high level of crew training. In any case, things changed when it was discovered that a conversion kit to cover both Mark IV and Mark VII versions of the Churchill was not feasible, and in the end it was agreed that Crocodile conversions should be limited to the new Mark VII. In practice, of course, this meant that the same conversion could be applied to the Mark VIII, which was essentially the Mark VII armed with a 95mm howitzer, although Crocodile versions of the Mark VIII are very rare. It is also quite likely that no Mark IV Churchill Crocodiles ever existed. Indeed it seems highly unlikely that field conversions were ever carried out. Late-production Churchills came complete with all the basic fittings necessary to convert into Crocodiles with a minimum of extra work, even down to holes, drilled and tapped into the machine-gun mounting, to which the armoured counterweight of the flame-projector could be bolted.

In fact, as the War Office soon realized, it made a lot more sense to dedicate specific regiments to operate the Crocodiles rather than simply spread them around to all and sundry. This policy came as a considerable surprise to the first regiment so dedicated: 7th Battalion The Buffs (otherwise known as the Royal East Kent Regiment), for the duration of the war to be known as 141st Regiment, RAC, was doing gunnery training in their Churchill tanks at Warcop when the commanding officer and the intelligence officer were summoned to London. They returned with news that the regiment would be converting to operate flamethrowers and that speed was of the essence. Some of them would be required to go ashore on D-Day, which was just ten weeks away.

According to an anonymous chronicler of 141st RAC, Crocodile training was confined both in terms of time and space available. Although 79th Armoured Division was not involved with flamethrowers at this time, it is probable that 43rd Royal Tank Regiment, which was the division's experimental regiment, may have done some of the initial work. But according to The Buffs much of this training proved to be wrong, at least at the outset. An officer who wrote some initial historical notes says that they trained to attack buildings and strongpoints, but in Normandy the regiment spent most of its time dealing with woods, trenches and similar obstacles.

The regiment was in fact suffering from precisely those difficulties that had been anticipated with the other 'Funnies' administered by 79th Armoured Division. For example, 141st RAC assumed that it knew best about the operational employment of flamethrowers and found that it was constantly in conflict with divisional commanders who were also trained to believe that they knew best about everything. In particular, it was difficult to make infantry understand that they needed to stay up close with the Crocodiles and actually advance through the flame to take advantage of the initial shock. Furthermore, one should not forget that, as part of the original design, the Crocodile was also a fighting tank, and that may well have been a tactical mistake.

On 14 June 1944 (D-Day + 8) three Crocodiles of 15 Troop, 141st RAC, advanced on the occupied village of La Senaudiere in Normandy on the incorrect understanding that British infantry were about to attack. Instead, the three Churchills found themselves sharing the village with German tanks. One, a Panther, put two rounds through a Crocodile trailer that, contrary to expectations, did

...ping up the trailer with ...ne fuel was also hard work. ... bulk of the fuel was poured ...ight from 45-gallon (204-litre) ...ms when possible, but in ...on every drop was precious ...t was essential to fill it ...t up to the top, another ...k-breaking duty.

not burn, but one Crocodile was later lost and went up in flames very quickly. Fear of fire was the normal condition for most tank men, but in the Crocodile it had an extra dimension. It was hardly surprising that the regiment felt ill used and it was also suffering from too much dispersion.

As a regular Churchill regiment the 141st was trained to fight as an entity or at least in squadron strength, but now that everyone wanted a few Crocodiles, even when the rest of the regiment arrived in France later in June, it would often find itself spread across a three-division front, fighting as individual troops. Certain details aside, the organization was based on an armoured regiment in a tank brigade: that is three squadrons, each responsible for five troops each of three Crocodiles, one of which in each troop would be equipped with an extra No.19 radio set to act as a Control Tank.

Two troopers, with their cap badges conveniently blotted out by the censor (but probabl[y] 141st RAC), demonstrate that fitting pressure cylinders, all f[our] of them, into a Crocodile traile[r] is no easy task.

To begin with 141st RAC was something of an orphan among the armoured units in France, although more or less under the control of 31st Army Tank Brigade. This relationship was formalized in August 1944, and then in September the 141st became part of the all-embracing 79th Armoured Division. This organization made a great deal of sense, since Crocodiles could be classed as 'Funnies' the same as Flail tanks or Armoured Vehicle Royal Engineers (AVREs). They also needed the same kind of administrative control to reduce the incidence of poor employment. Divisional commanders who believed they had the authority to retain the Crocodiles once a specific operation was over soon learned that a 79th Armoured Division advisor had what amounted to absolute power over the loaned equipment and was not to be tangled with. Not that this helped with the regiment's desire to fight as a body, indeed it made it worse. From October 1944 the squadron organization was modified so that it now comprised three troops, each of four Crocodiles and a fourth troop of three. The reason was that now it would be possible, at least in the majority of cases, to field half-troops of just two Crocodiles when required. However, the pressure this created on Crocodile crews was eased to some extent in October, when a second Crocodile regiment joined the brigade in the form of 1st Fife & Forfar Yeomanry.

By this time, naturally, 141st RAC had accumulated a great deal of experience, not only in dozens of minor actions but in at least two major ones. In the first, B Squadron, at the request of General Omar Bradley, supported the US Ninth Army in an attack on the fortified port of Brest. Then in September 1944 Operation *Astonia*, the attack on Le Havre, involved most of the regiment in a massive and highly formalized assault embracing all the resources of 79th Armoured Division.

Lessons learned

'Lessons learned' is a popular military phrase – often quoted, sometimes heeded. From the point of view of the Crocodiles, there was a lot to learn.

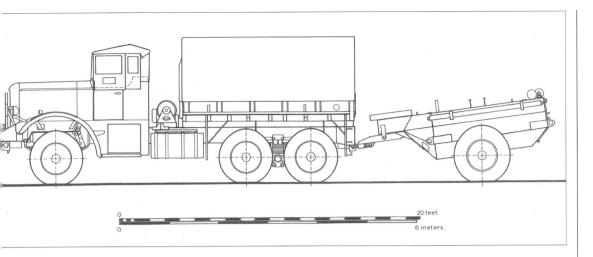

20 feet
6 meters.

chard Harley's drawing of a ocodile trailer being towed a Mack NM6. This was a -wheel drive truck in the 6-ton ss issued to the British Army a Medium Artillery Tractor, a e that it shared with the AEC tador 4x4, which it sometimes o supplanted.

In action, for example, crews soon realized how important it was to shield the trailer as much as possible with the tank. Armoured to withstand nothing more potent than small-arms fire the trailer was a very vulnerable item. Both driver and commander were constantly aware that it must not be exposed to enemy fire and there was need for considerably more manoeuvring than the crew of an ordinary tank needed to worry about.

There was also the business of preparing for action. It is not known how often the special pump was used, but it soon became normal practice to fill the containers in each trailer direct from 45-gallon (204-litre) drums. A framework of scaffolding pipes was constructed so that the drums could be rolled direct from the transporting lorry to a position above the trailer and the liquid poured straight in, topping up being done from smaller drums. But that was only the half of the procedure; next came the job of pressuring up. Gradually, carefully, the five pressure cylinders were turned on (nitrogen was now preferred to compressed air). Do it too quickly and one was liable to damage many of the valves and piping. That done, however, it was imperative to get into action as soon as possible. During training one officer from 141st RAC had referred to the Crocodile trailer as a mobile air leak, and if the action was delayed for any time pressure would steadily drop until the flame fuel emerged as a pathetic trickle. If that happened the tank would have to withdraw from action while the crew went through the back-breaking process of replacing the cylinders. It called for fine judgement and, as best they could, crews liked to wait until they were within about 30 minutes of action before turning on the pressure. At least in the Carriers, where the pressure cylinders were handy, one could more or less turn them on or off at will.

For long-distance moves, such as the journey to Brest undertaken by B Squadron, 141st RAC, the tanks went by transporter while the trailers were towed by lorries. Each squadron was provided with 15 AEC Matador Medium Artillery Tractors for this role, but written accounts indicate that when they were available the big Mack NM6 tractors were used because the unsprung, unbraked trailers could be quite a handful on the road. There is also some evidence to suggest that M3 half-tracks, of which each squadron had three, could be used, possibly to recover abandoned trailers from the battlefield.

Canadian Wasps

The Canadians accepted British developments with Carriers such as the Wasp II up to a point, but they were not sold on the need to put the fuel tanks under armour. They wanted to maintain the general utility of the Universal Carrier and decided to install a 75-gallon (340-litre) container crosswise, outside the armour at the back. The result was designated the Wasp IIC. In most other respects the two types were identical, but the Canadians saw two advantages to their design. In the first place it meant that the Wasp IIC could be used, to a certain extent, as a regular Carrier without having to dismantle all the flame equipment. They also pointed out that, even in the flamethrower role, the vehicle's ability to carry a third crew member in the rear, on the left side of the engine, meant that he could use a light machine gun or a 2-in. mortar, in addition to acting as an observer able to spot things that the driver or flame operator might miss.

Canada also developed a new Carrier flamethrower, which they called the Barracuda. Reginald Fraser examined the drawings for the PWD and reported to Banks in March 1943. He was not very impressed. The flame-gun, which he said was reputedly the Barracuda's best feature, was simply a modified Cockatrice and he doubted if it could meet the claims made on its behalf for range. A few days later a comparative trial was arranged between a prototype Barracuda and what Fraser referred to as a Wasp III – which we assume was in fact the Mark II. He told Banks that any suggestion that the two designs should be amalgamated was not a good idea: 'I can only suggest that the Barracuda is a badly brought-up child of too near a relationship for legal marriage!'

The first recorded employment of the Wasp II in action occurred in late July or early August 1944 near Hill 112 in Normandy. The organization of Carriers in conventional infantry battalions and the more specialized motor battalions is covered in New Vanguard 110: *Universal Carrier 1936–48* and it seems reasonable to assume that, for flame operations at least, a section of three Carriers would be fitted with Wasp equipment. Even so, on this scale flame was very much a weapon of opportunity and it would make sense that every battalion, once convinced of the value of flame, would maintain at least one section ready for action at all times.

A Wasp IIC on a railway wagon. This example has panels of the so-called plastic armour applied both inside and out around the crew compartment at the front.

24

A1: AEC Heavy Pump Unit, 1941

A2: AEC Basilisk, Southall, 1942

A

B

B1: Infantry Tank Mark III, Valentine. Ministry of Supply flamethrower design, Langhurst, March 1942

B2: Churchill Mark II Oke flamethrower *Beetle* of 8 Troop, B Squadron, 14th Canadian Army Tank Regiment, Dieppe, 19 August 1942

C1: Wasp II Carrier, 1st Battalion Highland Light Infantry, 53rd Welsh Division, Normandy, July 1944

C2: Wasp IIC Carrier, Westminster Regiment, 5th Canadian Armoured Division, Italy, 16 December 1944

C

D: CHURCHILL MARK VII CROCODILE FLAMETHROWER AND TRAILER

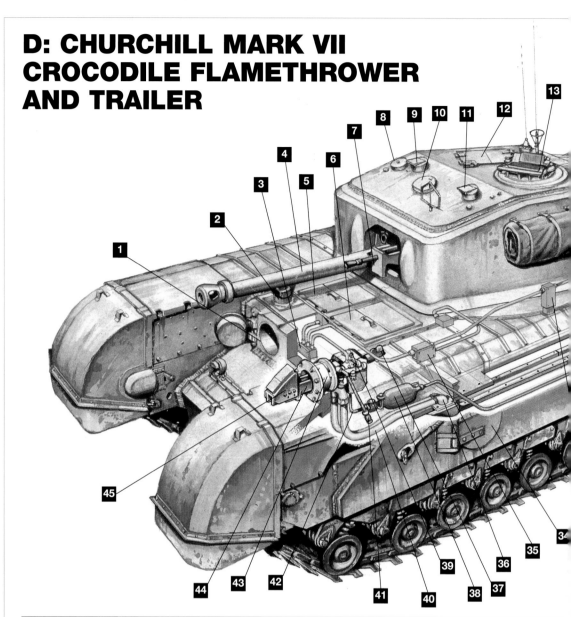

KEY

1 Driver's aperture
2 Driver's periscope
3 Driver's control box
4 75mm main armament
5 Driver's hatch
6 Flame gunner's hatch
7 Co-axial machine gun
8 Two-inch (50.8mm) smoke-bomb thrower
9 Loader's periscope
10 Turret ventilator
11 Gunner's periscope
12 Loader's hatch
13 Commander's hatch
14 Ethyl bromide fire extinguisher
15 Towing Link support bracket

16 Jettison block
17 Trailer jettison release gear
18 Main control valve
19 Control panel
20 Compressed air cylinders
21 Manhandling tube.
22 Flame fuel tanks
23 Rear access door opening
24 Manhandling tube socket
25 Drain valve
26 Fuel valve
27 Trailer support leg
28 Spill box
29 Rear Link
30 Front Link

31 Rear junction box
32 Fuel pipe conduit
33 Commander's control box
34 Side hull door
35 Flame gunner's control box
36 Deflector (where fuel pipe enters hull)
37 Flame gun trigger
38 Low pressure gas reservoir
39 Flame gun controller
40 Flame fuel pipes
41 Flame gun direction control handle
42 Gas pipe
43 Flame gun ball mounting
44 Flame gun cradle
45 Counterweight

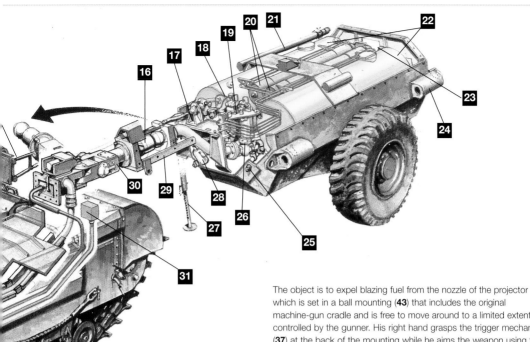

PECIFICATIONS

w: five
mbat weight: 45 tons 15 cwt. (46,484kg)
rall length: 40ft 6.½ in. (12.3m)
lth: 10ft 8in. (3.2m)
ght: 8ft 2in. (2.4m)
ine: Bedford Twin-Six 350bhp
nsmission: Merritt-Brown H41
l capacity (Churchill tank): 150 gallons (682 litres)
ximum speed: 13.5mph (21km/h)
ximum range: 90 miles (144k)
l consumption: 0.6mpg (0.2k/l)
ding depth (unprepared): 3ft 4in. (1m)
nament: 75mm Mark V & 7.92mm Besa MG
munition: 84 rounds
zzle Velocity: 2,030fps (618m)
ective range: 2,000 yards (1,828m)
n elevation/depression: 20 deg/12.5 deg
me fuel capacity: 400 gallons (1,818 litres)
ration of fire: 4.7 gallons (21 litres) per second
ective range: 110 yards (100.5m)

The object is to expel blazing fuel from the nozzle of the projector which is set in a ball mounting (**43**) that includes the original machine-gun cradle and is free to move around to a limited extent, controlled by the gunner. His right hand grasps the trigger mechanism (**37**) at the back of the mounting while he aims the weapon using the long arm (**41**), reaching outwards to the left.

Bearing in mind that red represents sections of the tank cut away to reveal detail then yellow shows the plumbing associated with fuel supply, blue the piping for compressed air and pale green the electrical circuitry required to ignite the fuel. On the trailer, with the upper armour removed, we can see two large fuel containers (**22**) and the compressed air cylinders (**20**) sandwiched between them. A complex network of pipes carries the pressurized air into a system of valves and filters that provide propulsion for the fuel mixture which, by means of a large-diameter pipe, now passes through a series of universal joints known as The Link (**29/30**), which connects the Crocodile trailer to the tank. At this point the fuel is directed downwards, at the rear of the tank and, mostly in a protective duct, beneath the hull until it re-enters, through a hole in the floor protected by a deflector (**36**). Here the fuel pipe splits in two so that unexpended fuel can be circulated back through the system, although at this stage it is not under serious pressure. Meanwhile another, smaller pipe, also passing through The Link delivers compressed air to a reservoir (**38**) situated close to the flame gunner's seat. There is no electrical connection with the trailer but there is an independent circuit around the tank that carries power from the tank's own system, aided by its auxiliary generator as required and via a series of control boxes available to certain crew members, to a final junction at the front, including two coils which generate the ignition spark. Here it all comes together, along with a supply of petrol pumped from the Churchill's own fuel tank, which initiates ignition. In reality the rear end of the projector would be covered by a shield in order to protect the flame gunner but this is not shown in the interests of clarity. The Link is an impressive combination of considerable strength, remarkable flexibility but very fine engineering that enables fuel to pass from the trailer to the tank no matter how many twists and turns the pair undergo, nor what strain the junction may be under on very difficult ground. Yet, at the same time, should it prove necessary to ditch the trailer in a hurry this was easily done with the loss of only a few drops of fuel. Once separated from the trailer, and as time permitted, the segment of towing Link still attached to the rear of the Churchill could be folded aside and secured by a special bracket (**15**).

E: Churchill VII Crocodile, B Squadron, 1st Fife & Forfar Yeomanry, River Rhine, March 1945

E

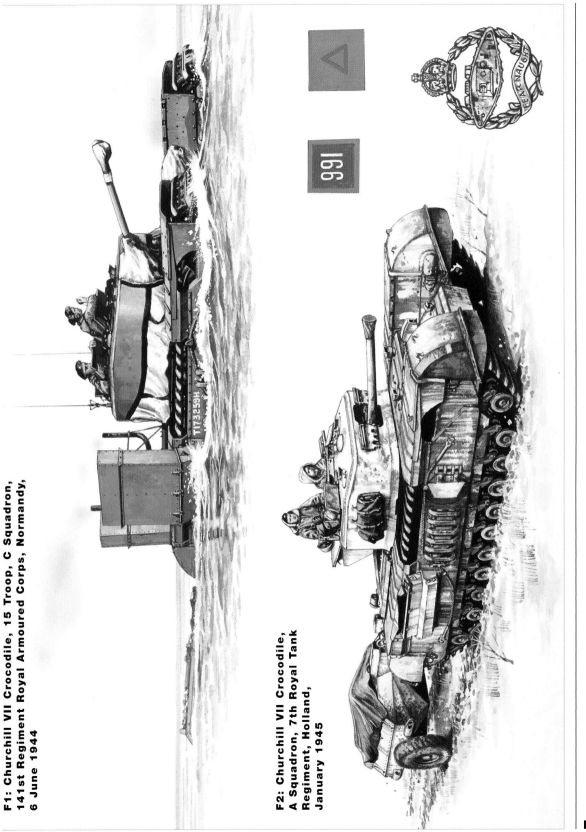

F1: Churchill VII Crocodile, 15 Troop, C Squadron, 141st Regiment Royal Armoured Corps, Normandy, 6 June 1944

F2: Churchill VII Crocodile, A Squadron, 7th Royal Tank Regiment, Holland, January 1945

F

G1: M4A4 Sherman V Adder prototype

G2: LVT IV Sea Serpent, Amphibian Support Regiment, Royal Marines, Studland Bay, Dorset, 1945

This option would certainly become easier after August 1944 when the Canadian Wasp IIC became available. Definitive evidence is wanting, but it seems likely that Wasp equipment was issued as supplies arrived in theatre, so that British battalions could be found operating the Canadian Wasp IIC and vice versa. While the Crocodile, by its very nature, was best suited to formal, pre-planned attacks, the Wasps appear to have been employed on a more immediate basis. For example, a nest of enemy machine guns, tucked into a hedgerow, would be an ideal target. While one or two guns might suffer the full treatment of flame, the rest would rapidly evacuate the area as soon as the flame started to belch forth.

The Crocodiles expand

Like other elements of 79th Armoured Division the Crocodiles soon attracted the attention of the division's inventive engineers. Trials were conducted with Crocodiles towing stores sledges, or even gutted Universal Carriers as stores trailers behind the fuel trailer, which must have been a driver's nightmare. Another idea was to use flame to cook-off and explode German *Schu* mines. A Crocodile was tested for this purpose, but it did not work.

The revived 7th RTR (it had been 10th RTR until April 1943) was the third Churchill regiment to convert to Crocodiles. This took place in February 1945, shortly after the regiment had withdrawn from its part in the investment of Dunkirk. In their training they were assisted by 1st Fife & Forfar Yeomanry. So, for the final four months of the war in Europe, 31st Armoured Tank Brigade included three Crocodile regiments. Not that it ever operated as a complete brigade, or its constituent regiments even as complete regiments come to that. To pick an extreme example, one gets the impression that 1st Fife & Forfar Yeomanry invariably had one squadron supporting elements of the US Army who, by now, seem to have become totally sold on flamethrowers.

The Americans had shown a lot of interest in flame early in 1944, when a Committee on Special Equipment reported to General Eisenhower that Britain would be able to supply equipment to convert 100 Sherman tanks to the Crocodile role, starting in March 1944. It appears to have been an optimistic promise, for although a prototype was soon ready, on an M4A4 (Sherman V) tank, the supply of trailers alone was bound to interfere with

British requirements. The Sherman Crocodile was arguably a somewhat clumsier conversion than the Churchill due to its design and, in order to keep things simple, the Churchill-type trailer was used and the same coupling but from there everything was external. The flame fuel pipe ran along the right side of the hull in an armoured cover and was connected to a projector located on the sloping hull front plate, close to the hull machine-gunner's position.

Subsequently, American interest declined. The idea of tanks pulling trailers did not appeal and, until the assault on Brest, the activities of British Crocodiles did not inspire them. On the other hand, attempts to employ an American-designed tank flamethrower in Normandy were dismissed as pathetic, so interest in the British design was rekindled and four M4 Crocodiles delivered to 739th Tank Battalion in November 1944. They formed a special platoon, but despite requests no more were ordered and their use was limited. Even so, there is evidence that British attempts to improve the design continued after the war and included an amphibious, DD version.

In Italy, where the writ of 79th Armoured Division did not run, it was arranged to kill off the 25th Army Tank Brigade and recreate it as 25th Armoured Engineer Brigade, composed of RAC and Royal Engineer (RE) elements. Although this formation was not officially created until March 1945, most of its constituent regiments had been undergoing conversion a good deal earlier and the one that interests us, 51st Royal Tank Regiment, learned that it would be operating Churchill Crocodiles and Sherman Crab flail tanks. It finally settled on A and C Squadrons for the former which, in keeping with typical Crocodile practice, were subdivided in half-squadrons named Green and Black in A Squadron, Red and Blue in C Squadron.

At first few opportunities arose to test the flame weapon in action, and the Crocodiles seem to have remained on stand-by most of the time. The same seems to have been true of the Wasp Carriers with the infantry. The Canadians say that before 16 December 1944 it had not been possible to bring the Wasps up in time to take part in any actions.

An M4A4 Sherman V fitted with what appears to be a wooden mock-up of the Sherman Crocodile equipment. This was an odd decision in a sense, since the US Army, for whom it was intended, would not use the M4A4 in action if they had any choice in the matter.

However, on that date the Westminster Regiment of 5th Canadian Armoured Division employed four Wasps against German positions on the far bank of the Munio Canal, as a result of which the crossing at this point was virtually unopposed.

This action, however, pales into insignificance when compared with the use of flame in support of the crossing of the Senio river on 9 April 1945. Following a massive barrage of bombs and artillery, 28 Churchill Crocodiles and 127 Wasps took up positions on top of the friendly flood bank, spaced roughly 70 yards (64m) apart along a 5-mile (8km) front. They poured out such a deluge of flame that 2nd New Zealand Division, supported by C Squadron 51st RTR, suffered no fatalities at all during the crossing. For the remaining weeks of the campaign in Italy flame was in favour all round but in particular with New Zealand, Indian and Polish forces.

Out East

The potential value of flamethrowing tanks for use in the Far East was quickly appreciated in Britain, but based upon recent experience, particularly in Burma, it was agreed that a trailer would not be a good idea on grounds of manoeuvrability and that a Carrier would be a liability because it lacked overhead cover.

Late in 1943 the PWD, in conjunction with the DTD, proposed a light tank flamethrower, perhaps along similar lines to contemporary American developments. Whether this implied that the light tanks would be American Stuarts or earlier and smaller British types is uncertain, but the former would seem to be more likely. The authorities also stated a preference for cordite rather than gas as the source of pressure since, they reasoned, heavy gas cylinders would be very difficult to transport and handle in jungle conditions. Not that any of this mattered very much. The project was dropped early in 1944 when it was concluded that a more heavily armoured tank would be more suitable so, under the code-name 'Salamander', another project was initiated involving Sherman and Churchill tanks.

The Salamander scheme is not worth studying in great detail since, despite evolving into nine different designs of considerable complexity, it was ultimately dropped. Even so, a rough outline helps to indicate how people were thinking at the time. No trailer was to be used and the flame fuel had to be carried within the tank, under armour. At first it was hoped to install the flame-projector in a fully rotating turret, still retaining the main armament, but this proved impossible and most of the later designs involved a flamethrower replacing, but usually disguised as, the main gun. Naturally this meant that the installation would be permanent. Cordite

A version of the Sherman Salamander in which the 75mm gun is replaced by what is described as a 'Long Wasp' flame-projector.

...herman V (M4A4) Adder with ...last weights to represent ...wage is hoisted clear of the ...und by a crane, probably to ...ablish the centre of gravity. ... details of the additions refer ...he colour plates. Surviving ...lications also refer to an ...A2 (Sherman III) version ...Adder.

propulsion was rejected since it could not generate sufficient pressure and the majority of versions would have used CO_2. The endless succession of designs rather implies indecision, but in any case the scheme was defeated because of difficulties in producing a safe rotary base junction. The entire scheme was closed down by the end of 1944. Incidentally, the Churchill was only included as an alternative on the first design. All the rest were based on Shermans.

Whether the 'Adder' project began as a result of the demise of Salamander or independently in its own right is not clear, but it was different to the extent that the Adder was a bolt-on arrangement intended to be fitted to a tank as required, at a base workshop if need be. It had much more in common with the old Churchill Oke than anything else and the armoured cover, shielding an 80-gallon (363-litre) fuel container and pressure cylinder at the rear, is almost identical. The rear housing, armoured to 0.55in. (14mm), also contained the various valves and controls, although the master switch could be activated by the flame-gunner. He sat alongside the driver at the front. The hull machine gun was removed but the flame-projector, which had a 180-degree arc of fire, was mounted in place of the periscope in the hatch above the gunner's head and it was fed by a pipe, in an armoured cover, that ran from the tank at the back, along the edge of the hull and through the hull just to the right of this hatch. The weapon had an effective range of 80 yards (73m).

As before, with the Far East in mind the original plan was to develop Adder for the Sherman and the Mamba (later renamed Cobra) for the Churchill. Parts were to be interchangeable as far as possible, but Adder took priority because Shermans were already operational in the Far East whereas Churchills were not. Although 500 kits were ordered the Adder was still not ready when the war ended, but development continued, including an improved version again designed for both the Sherman and Churchill, for issue to India.

One cannot leave this region without mentioning two Australian contributions, the Frog and Murray, although they are covered in more detail in New Vanguard 8: *Matilda Infantry Tank 1938–45*. Perhaps less well known was Sea Serpent, a British modification to the American Landing Vehicle Tracked (LVT) Mark IV, known as the Buffalo in British service. In 1945 the Royal Marines formed the 34th Amphibian Support Regiment, largely from members of the old Royal Marine Armoured Support Group, supplemented by specialist Army personnel. Transferred to India early in 1945 it was to be equipped with the American LVT (A)4, mounting a 75mm howitzer in the turret, a rocket-firing version and the Sea Serpent itself – the basic LVT IV that mounted a pair of Wasp projectors and an additional Browning machine gun. The war ended before the regiment had a chance to employ its amphibious equipment, but it returned to Britain after the war and remained as a Combined Operations demonstration unit until 1947.

Just to illustrate the amazing versatility of the Wasp, it might be worth recording here that the Royal Electrical & Mechanical Engineers (REME) adapted it to fit the little M29C Weasel amphibian (a device that was more or less copied by the French for use in Indo-China). Most bizarre of all, No.1 Demolition Squadron, commanded by Vladimir Peniakoff, managed to fit one to a Jeep.

Hill-climbing trials at Chaklala, India, on 2 April 1946. The Churchill was always a good climber, but it was not regarded as suitable for the Far East on account of the trailer. Even so, some 250 units were earmarked for use in Burma if the Japanese had not surrendered when they did.

THE FLAME GOES OUT

Considering the enthusiasm expressed about the value of flame by so many influential individuals at the end of the war, its rapid disappearance from the scene is difficult to explain. Maybe, under the threat of nuclear war, the flash from a bit of blazing petrol was hardly noticed.

Not that flame was extinguished at once. In August 1946 *The Tank* (the RTR journal) republished an article that first appeared in a Royal Air Force magazine concerning a demonstration laid on for a party of RAF officers by 7th RTR in Germany. It involved a mock flamethrower attack that certainly made a striking impression, although it is often the case that members of one service find the activities of another either baffling or awe-inspiring. Yet by the time this article appeared, 7th RTR was in India operating light tanks and armoured cars, while the rump of 79th Armoured Division, now known as the Specialised Armour Establishment (SAE), continued to experiment and improve the equipment.

As far as flamethrowers were concerned, SAE, when it issued its final report in 1951, was trying out various improvements to the Crocodile. These included a remote-control method of pressuring up, a pressure gauge for the flame-gunner and an offset sighting telescope that would not be obscured by flame and smoke. The Sea Serpent flamethrowing amphibian was still being tested (now under the designation FV502) and attempts were being made to create a DD swimming version of the Sherman Crocodile (see New Vanguard 123: *Swimming Shermans*). Once SAE was disbanded its role was to be taken over by 7th RTR again, now based at Bovington, which became responsible for all of those examples of specialized armour operated by the RAC. Yet it becomes clear, reading between the lines, that the plan was to make flame available to all armoured regiments rather then employing dedicated regiments as was done during the war.

In the intervening years 7th RTR had been busy. Late in 1950 C Squadron, equipped with Crocodiles, had been shipped out to Pusan as part of the British contribution to the United Nations force in Korea. It took quite a while to get everything together and in fact the squadron never operated as a flamethrower unit. Trailers were detached and for the time that they were there the Churchills only ever operated as gun tanks.

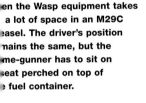

en the Wasp equipment takes a lot of space in an M29C easel. The driver's position mains the same, but the me-gunner has to sit on seat perched on top of e fuel container.

The Director Royal Armoured Corps (DRAC) used to publish what were known as Liaison Letters, which kept everyone up to date on developments. One issue that came out shortly after the war contained a brief note on flamethrowers. It announced that the Churchill Crocodile would be the main weapon for the immediate future, with a few Sherman Adders in India, while work on the Sherman Crocodile would be suspended and the design of the Churchill Cobra abandoned. But most interesting of all, it went on to say that since Cromwell, Comet and Centurion regiments would not have integral flame equipment it would be necessary to issue Churchill Crocodiles.

There is, in theory, no obvious reason why Crocodile equipment could not be applied to these tanks since, suspension systems aside, the basic hull form was much the same. Granted the Cromwell was already cramped inside and should in any case be phased out of service very soon, but there was not a great deal wrong with Comet in the late 1940s, and of course Centurion was the coming thing. In fact there is evidence, in the shape of one photograph, that a Comet Crocodile existed. No date is given and, beyond the fact that it is towing a trailer, no evidence to prove whether it was in fact complete and able to flame. It may have been no more than an experimental test rig – such a thing is known because a report survives concerning a trial in which a Crocodile trailer, attached to a Comet, was towed at speed (well, 8mph/12.8km/h) over a series of obstacles to see what happened. The trailer appears to have spent most of its time airborne and bounced with such violence that it finally broke away from the tank and went off on its own. Maybe this was the reason why the fast cruiser tanks were not considered suitable as Crocodiles. But what of the Centurion?

Originally the idea was rejected because it cut down the amount of ammunition that the tank could carry. In any case, there was a rival. Based on a firm 21st Army Group requirement, a heavier tank designated A45 was on the drawing board, probably better known as the Universal Tank, in response to Field Marshal Montgomery's oft-expressed wishes. The idea was to fit the tank with a built-in power take-off so that all manner of attachments and adaptations could be employed. In the case of a flamethrower this would be a pump, operating a Crocodile-type projector mounted on the co-driver's hatch. This projector would traverse to give an arc of fire of 120 degrees. DRAC insisted that a trailer with a capacity of about 400 gallons (1,818 litres) was essential.

By 1946 the A45 designation had been changed to FV201, but as the peacetime economy kicked in many of the features were trimmed and a number had been rejected before the first mild steel pilots appeared. The project was officially dropped in 1948, although a drawing described as FV201 (Flame Thrower) dated October 1949 survives. This, in turn, rejuvenated the Centurion project and a Mark 3 tank was put aside for conversion, albeit with an old Churchill Crocodile trailer. The projector was mounted on top of the hull at the front and the problem next to be solved was who in the crew should operate it? Trials were conducted throughout 1953 and 1954. To begin with they offered the job to the commander, but his vision while closed down proved inadequate. Next they tried the driver, but he was always cutting himself on the control switch and found it difficult to drive and work the flame-gun at the same time. Finally they turned to the loader who had a good view and nothing else to do. The trouble was that with the tank moving he was thrown about all over the place, which did not help his aim. The obvious answer might have been to install another crew position alongside the driver, as they did with the Centurion AVRE, but this was not accepted. Maybe it would have reduced ammunition stowage to an unacceptable level, but the chances are that it was an economic decision: the budget would not run to such a drastic conversion.

e Sea Serpent prepares for a
nonstration at Studland Bay
Dorset, while a gaggle of
servers prepare to follow it
o Poole Bay and witness
nts from a DUKW.

In post-war Canada, flame was still regarded as a viable weapon and an improved version of the Wasp IIC, known as the Iroquois, was taken into service. It was described as being cheaper, simpler and lighter than the Wasp with a capacity of 80 gallons (363 litres) and a range of 190–200 yards (173–182m) in good conditions. The best feature, as described by a Canadian report, was the way in which the flame fanned out when it was fired. Even so, the need for greater protection, which had already manifested itself during the war in the shape of the Ram Badger, was now fulfilled by a late-production M4A2 Sherman III hull. This operated without a turret and with a Wasp IIC projector installed in the front machine-gun position. Also known as the Badger, it was a self-contained

The dubious Comet Crocodile. It may have been nothing more than a tank and trailer combination created to try out the effect of speed on towed trailers. There is no evidence of a flame-projector at the hull machine-gun position.

The Ram Badger was a Canadian modification. Wasp projectors were installed in place of the hull machine gun in late-production Rams, indicated here by the arrow. However, this example also has a projector, protected by a shield mounted on top of the hull.

The Crocodile trailer, towed by a Comet, becomes airborne during towing trials over a prepared course.

it with a creditable performance, but when it was demonstrated in Canada in June 1949 the report was annotated by one officer 'I would not ask troops to go into battle sitting on top of 150 gallons [681 litres] of fuel,' and in the event only three prototypes were built.

The final chapter in the British flamethrower saga concerns a period, starting in the 1950s, when a vast range of potential weapons came up for consideration, all identified in part by a colour: Orange William, Green Archer and Blue Steel are among the better known. At least three were flamethrowers – there was Red Cyclops, about which nothing is known, and Red Hermes, which is described as a trailer-type unit capable of attachment to various British Armoured Fighting Vehicles (AFVs). The fuel of this unit, in the form of thickened petrol, and pressurizing gas consisting of carbon dioxide dissolved in acetone, shared a common tank but were separated by a flexible membrane. Operating pressure was 400psi and the effective range about 200 yards (182m). There was also Blue Perseus, which again involved a trailer, this time for a medium tank, and contained both fuel and propellant held apart by a membrane but in such a way that 400 gallons (1,818 litres) of fuel occupied the centre, surrounded by compressed air. The performance figures were calculated as being similar to those of Red Hermes. And at the very last there was a return to a cordite-operated system, as discarded in 1942. This one does not appear to have qualified for an exotic code-name and it turned out to be of such complexity that it was never developed, but the plan was to produce a system that would fit inside an AFV and deliver flame up to a range of 100 yards (91.4m).

As each of these projects died, the popularity of flame as a weap
seems to have decreased. Only the US Army kept the faith and still h
flamethrowing versions of the M113 Armoured Personnel Carrier (AF
operational in Vietnam at least up to 1969. Maybe, in peacetime, we fi
the idea of burning men alive a bit too unpleasant to contempla
although if wartime evidence is any guide flame was more deterrent th
killer, except in the case of the most fanatical resisters. Possibly it v
simply more trouble and more risk than it was worth. Whatever the ca
it had its day and is now gone.

BIBLIOGRAPHY

Anon, *A Squadron Diary 7th Royal Tank Regiment* (1945)
Anon, *The Story of 79th Armoured Division* (1945)
Anon, *79th Armoured Division Final Report* (1945)
Anon, *A Short History of the 51st Royal Tank Regiment*, C.M.F. (1946)
Anon, *Contribution to Victory*, AEC Ltd (*c.* 1946)
Anon, *Final Report of the Specialised Armour Establishment Royal Armoured Corps*, War Office (1951)
Knight, Colonel C. R. B., *Historical Record of The Buffs Royal East Kent Regiment 1919–1948*, The Medici Society (1951)
Sellar, R. J. B., *The Fife and Forfar Yeomanry 1919–1956*, William Blackwood & Sons (1960)
Townsin, Alan, *AEC*, Ian Allan (1998)
Wilson, Andrew, *Flame Thrower*, William Kimber (1956)

The only surviving diagram showing the flame-throwing version of FV201, essentially a Centurion turret on what would become the Conqueror chassis. The flamethrower variant was to have a small turret ahead of the main one, operated by a crew member located to the left of the driver.

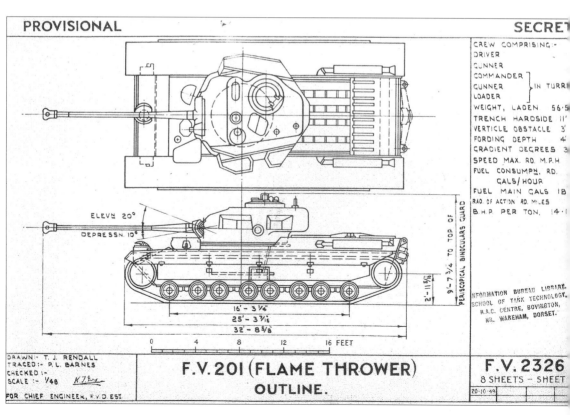

PROVISIONAL   SECRE

CREW COMPRISING:-
DRIVER
GUNNER
COMMANDER
GUNNER   IN TURRE
LOADER
WEIGHT, LADEN 56·5
TRENCH HARDSIDE 11'
VERTICLE OBSTACLE 3'
FORDING DEPTH   4'
GRADIENT DEGREES 3
SPEED MAX. RD. M.P.H
FUEL CONSUMPN. RD.
          GALS/HOUR
FUEL MAIN GALS 18
RAD. OF ACTION RD. MILES
B.H.P. PER TON. 14·1

ELEVN 20°
DEPRESSN 10°

INFORMATION BUREAU LIBRARY,
SCHOOL OF TANK TECHNOLOGY,
R.A.C. CENTRE, BOVINGTON,
NR. WAREHAM, DORSET.

16' - 3¼"
25' - 3⅞"
32' - 8⅝"

0   4   8   12   16 FEET

DRAWN:- T. J. RENDALL
TRACED:- P. L. BARNES
CHECKED :-
SCALE :- ¼8
FOR CHIEF ENGINEER, F.V.D.ESI

F.V. 201 (FLAME THROWER)
OUTLINE.

F.V. 2326
8 SHEETS – SHEET
20·10·49

COLOUR PLATE COMMENTARY

AEC HEAVY PUMP UNIT, 1941

...ing an official demonstration at Leeds Castle in Kent, this ...mp-operated system discharged flame fuel through its ...n projector at a range of 100 yards (91.4m) at the rate of ... gallons (3,409 litres) per minute. Fuel was carried in a ...e tank at the back, but no capacity is given. The small, ...iliary projector had a range of 75 yards (68.5m). The main ...ector, which is sometimes shown with a curved shield, ...ld be elevated to the vertical position to discourage low-...ng aircraft but, at a similar demonstration for the Royal ...y, an American stunt pilot showed that it was perfectly ...e to fly an aircraft through flame. The chassis was the ...ular AEC Model 0854 six-wheel drive diesel. One source ...ms that 25 of these were built, but that cannot be ...firmed. The vehicle is shown in a khaki brown finish typical ...the period, but it never entered military service so no ...kings were applied.

AEC BASILISK, SOUTHALL, 1942

...C are reputed to have built their first armoured car as ...rivate venture in 1941. It subsequently entered service ...the Mark I, on a rear-engined version of the Matador ...ssis, type 0855. The Basilisk appears to have used the ...ne chassis but with a modified hull and turret. This, in ..., led to the development of the AEC 0856 chassis, with ...70bhp (127kW) engine that became the basis of the AEC ...rk II armoured car. Thus the Basilisk may be seen as a ...between the two. It was photographed in company ...n other mobile flamethrowers during demonstrations ...Moody Down, but is shown here in grey primer paint ...it would have looked on first being rolled out from ...C's Southall factory. A claim by AEC that development of ...Basilisk was halted by the end of the war would seem ...oe a fiction. The project was probably killed off when a ...n to include flamethrowers in armoured car regiments ...s dropped.

B1: INFANTRY TANK MARK III, VALENTINE. MINISTRY OF SUPPLY FLAMETHROWER DESIGN, LANGHURST, MARCH 1942

The tanks used for these experiments did not display numbers, but appear to have been of the Mark I type. Shown here at Langhurst, the MoS version is towing the second type of trailer design. Very few details appear to have survived of the internal arrangements of the trailer, or of the way it coupled up to the tank, although the flame projector was photographed in some detail. Traverse and elevation employed a gear train, apparently operated by remote control from the driver's position. Other photographs of this tank show it with a different pattern trailer and the main armament removed from the turret.

B2: CHURCHILL MARK II OKE FLAMETHROWER *BEETLE* OF 8 TROOP, B SQUADRON, 14TH CANADIAN ARMY TANK REGIMENT, DIEPPE, 19 AUGUST 1942

Beetle displays a comprehensive set of markings as it sits, disabled, on the beach at Dieppe with a track broken. T68875 is the tank's own War Department number and the red/white/red display a form of national identification. The gold maple leaf and ram insignia is that of 1st Canadian Army Tank Brigade. The 14th Canadian Army Tank Regiment (CATR), the Calgary Regiment, as junior regiment in the brigade, is identified by the number 175 on a divided blue over khaki rectangle: the blue square signifies B Squadron while the number 8 is that of the particular Troop to which *Beetle* belongs. The armoured container on the rear of the tank, which housed the flame fuel reservoir and pressure cylinders, proved a very convenient place to paint this array of markings, which would also be repeated at the front.

The last of the line, the prototype Centurion Crocodile. The front-end layout was rather clumsy, but the trailer was the conventional type.

The post-war variation of the Badger developed by the Canadians gives an impressive demonstration. It is tempting to suggest that this is a lot of tank to modify to the flamethrower role with no other offensive capability.

C1: WASP II CARRIER, 1ST BATTALION HIGHLAND LIGHT INFANTRY, 53RD WELSH DIVISION, NORMANDY, JULY 1944

It is an indication of the complexity of British Army organization that by 1944 a dedicated Scottish regiment should find itself a significant element in a Welsh infantry division. The white 57 on a red square tells us that 1st Highland Light Infantry (HLI) at this time was junior regiment in the first brigade (71st Brigade) of the division, whose famous Red W insignia adorns the Carrier's other track guard. It is believed that 1st HLI was the first ever to use Wasp flamethrowers in action, when they were supporting 2nd Battalion the Monmouthshire Regiment, from the same division, in fighting west of Caen.

C2: WASP IIC CARRIER, WESTMINSTER REGIMENT, 5TH CANADIAN ARMOURED DIVISION, ITALY, 16 DECEMBER 1944

The large flame fuel tank across the rear of this Canadian version of the Wasp also proved an ideal place to paint vehicle markings, but there is some doubt about those shown. When 5th Canadian Armoured Division arrived in Italy, the Westminster Regiment was its Motor Battalion and the markings shown are correct for that role. However, at one stage, in keeping with local practice, British and Common-wealth armoured divisions in Italy added a second infantry brigade to their strength because infantry proved to be more effective than armour in the prevailing conditions. Thus, at the time of this action, the Westminster Regiment was part of the newly created 12th Canadian Infantry Brigade. Unfortunately, it has not proved possible to establish beyond doubt the num-bering system employed for a second infantry brigade in an armoured division, because it was peculiar to Italy. If it followed the practice in infantry divisions then 60 on a green square might be appropriate, since the Westies were the senior regiment in their brigade. On the other hand, such markings may never have been applied, since the entire Canadian Corps in Italy transferred to northwest Europe shortly after this action and 12th Brigade ceased to exist.

D: CHURCHILL MARK VII CROCODILE FLAMETHROWER AND TRAILER

Essentially this tank is an Infantry Tank Mark IV, type A22F, final production version of the Churchill. It retains virtually the standard features of that tank including the 75mm gun co-axial Besa machine gun in the turret. The only differenc that the hull machine gun, at the front, alongside the driv position, is replaced by a flame projector. Since the interic the tank remains standard we have elected to show mo those hidden features that are peculiar to the flame-thro role. One of the most impressive features of the design the complicated Link which not only served a a draw between tank and trailer but also as a secure conduit for fla fuel and compressed air (see page 17).

E: CHURCHILL VII CROCODILE, B SQUADRON, 1ST FIFE & FORFAR YEOMANRY, RIVER RHINE, MARCH 1945

The US Ninth Army, operating immediately alongside Br and Canadian forces in the advance into Germany, m considerable use of Crocodiles, and in particular those B Squadron, 1st Fife & Forfar Yeomanry, in March 1945 of 31st Armoured Brigade, 79th Armoured Division. advantage of this proximity was that supplies of flame and pressure cylinders were easier to maintain.

We view the tank as it flames. Notice that divisic insignia and unit codes are repeated on the trailer. As second most senior armoured regiment in the 31st Armou Brigade (as formed in February 1945), 1st Fife & Forfar w 992 in white on a green square.

F1: CHURCHILL VII CROCODILE, 15 TROOP, C SQUADRON, 141ST REGIMENT ROYAL ARMOURED CORPS, NORMANDY, 6 JUNE 1944

Preparing a tank for deep wading, as from landing craf shore, was a long, tiresome and messy business. Ev hatch and orifice had to be sealed, every crack filled wi sticky, mastic compound and extensions added to air int and exhaust pipes. Special books were printed to ensure everything was done properly and the object, with all ty of vehicle, was to ensure that it could keep going w immersed in up to 6ft (1.8m) of water.

Three Crocodiles of 141st RAC were included in D-Day plan to come ashore at Le Hamel on Gold Bea where they unconsciously re-enacted events at Dieppe. C tank drowned when it took to the water, the second got it bogged down in a shell crater while the third, having ma it across the beach, broke a track. Virtually all markings below water level in this case, but the tank still present colourful sight with the silver, waterproof fabric around turret ring, mantlet and weapons. Tyres on the trailer wer large that it was almost buoyant.

F2: CHURCHILL VII CROCODILE, A SQUADRON, 7TH ROYAL TANK REGIMENT, HOLLAND, JANUARY 1945

The use of whitewash to camouflage tanks against a snc background was common but of dubious value on such la and noisy machines. In any case it has started to wash off Crocodile. A section of the trackguard alongside the turret deliberately been removed. Churchill crews discovered tha it was damaged and bent upwards this section of trackgu could prevent the turret from traversing. Whitewash has a applied to the Crocodile trailer, but this has been promised by a sheet of canvas laid to protect whatever owed there. All markings on the tank would have been erated by the whitewash, but as senior regiment in the ade the 7th RTR would show 991 on a green square and squadron symbols. No name is shown on this tank but it orth recording that in its new guise as 7th RTR the ment seems to have retained its old 10th RTR names, h all began with J.

M4A4 SHERMAN V ADDER PROTOTYPE

Sherman flamethrower, the Adder seems to have been uch more practical proposition than the Crocodile. It may have had the capacity of a Crocodile trailer, but it was h more self-contained and interfered very little with the ting capabilities of the tank. Eighty gallons (363 litres) of e fuel was carried in a hull extension made from 14mm 5-in.) armour plate, which also contained the pressure nder and valves. The fuel pipe, where it ran along the e of the hull, was also protected by an armoured duct e the flame-projector itself replaced the hull machine-ner's periscope. Modifications to the tank itself were mal. An additional grille was fitted on top of the hull at very back and one of the internal stowage bins had to be ed so that four rounds of 75mm ammunition were lost.

n the buildings of Belsen Camp blazing in the kground, the crew of a Wasp IIC belonging to Battalion, Somerset Light Infantry, 43rd Wessex sion, take a break. Notice how they have adorned their rier with spare links of tank track to enhance protection.

This was to make room for a flexible pipe that curved around inside the hull to connect up with the projector. The projector, incidentally, was fitted with a No.35 sighting telescope in place of the periscope. The tank, which has appliqué armour panels on the side, is finished in standard US olive drab and the only visible marking is the British War Department (WD) number T147340.

G2: LVT IV SEA SERPENT, AMPHIBIAN SUPPORT REGIMENT, ROYAL MARINES, STUDLAND BAY, DORSET, 1945

Since this unique regiment never got the chance to see action with its vehicles, the Sea Serpent is shown as it looked during trials in Britain, at a secure location near Poole Harbour on the south coast. The capacious hold of the Buffalo has been altered to fit a pair of Wasp flamethrowers with fuel tanks and pressure bottles at the front and a simple structure to hold a .30-in. Browning machine gun at the rear. The Wasp projectors were in small turrets, each open at the back, which could be rotated through a limited arc and fired independently. The machine gun appears to have been included for anti-aircraft defence. In service Sea Serpent would carry a crew of five.

The regiment's badge, which may have been worn as a shoulder flash, showed a fouled anchor in yellow on a red triangle, itself outlined in yellow along each side and super-imposed on a dark-blue shield. It is not clear when this was adopted since the regiment began as the Royal Marine Armoured Support Group, which landed on D-Day. It went out to India in 1945 and saw some action in an infantry role on Java, but returned to Britain in 1946 to become part of the School of Combined Operations at Fremington in north Devon.

INDEX